Where's Margaret?

A Soul Searching Adventure

Mary e. Stewart

Where's Margaret?
A Soul Searching Adventure
Copyright © 2016 by Mary e. Stewart

ISBN-13:   Paperback: 978-1-63524-754-1
            PDF: 978-1-63524-755-8
            ePub: 978-1-63524-756-5
            Kindle: 978-1-63524-757-2

Printed in the United States of America

LitFire
PUBLISHING

LitFire LLC
1-800-511-9787
www.litfirepublishing.com
order@litfirepublishing.com

Faith is Trusting What You Cannot See

~ Mary e. Stewart

Resilience is one of the most important

Qualities we can develop

Because surviving is not good enough

We deserve to thrive

~ Author unknown~

Mary e.Stewart

Where's Margaret...A soul searching adventure

"Many times in our lives we begin searching for the answers to questions we have no answers for. The searches come in all different forms regardless of age and each of us go about the search in different ways. Whether it is about religion, career, family or just self and growth. It all begins within ourselves in the very quiet moments when we are able to hear clearly through the thoughts in our mind. This is a story of one of my own Soul Searching Adventures and perhaps you may find a little of yourself in my words".

Mary e. Stewart

Mary e. Stewart

We are made up of many parts within ourselves that begins in early childhood and continues for all time. There is the physical, the mental and the spiritual. My belief is that it is all in place before we are born and we are still in our Mother's womb. All of the miracles that are taking place as we form and become that bright light that is born in innocence. We are all of those miracles.

When one looks into a baby's eyes and the far reaching looks they give to us in just a moment or perhaps a gaze that stays for a while it is an interesting   phenomenon. I understand that many people think a baby cannot "see" and only sees the dark shapes because their eyes have not physically completed, but I am not so sure I believe that at least in the spiritual sense. I remember the first time my "Croceofixxo" or Cross, one of my twin grandsons, stared into my eyes as I was holding him in my arms, he was only a minute old. He looked all around me and then back to my eyes with a very deep gaze, eyes wide open. It was pretty amazing and there was a connection I cannot explain. I always wonder what is happening in the brain at that time and the thoughts it is forming. The beliefs that are now just a tiny seed but which will grow and flower into a system that will begin to form the whole life of the baby.

Mary e. Stewart

So many things come into play, parents, environment, friends, and society in general. So many things that will influence and help mold the belief system of this perfect being. Memories being formed which later seem like a dream and our not knowing whether it was real or not. How can the difference be told and which way will we lean. Only time shows the results.

When I was very young, perhaps two or three I have some very vivid memories of particular instances that played a large part in my life and which helped me form some particular ideas of myself. Were they real or were they dreams, it does not matter they played an important part anyway. We are all the sum total of what has happened in our lives, the experiences, the perceptions, the joys, humor, sadness, anger, loneliness, feeling complete, being peaceful, and the thoughtful times.

Mary e.Stewart

Sometimes as children in our playtime we have friends that visit, friends that no one else is able to see but they are there nonetheless. Friends that we hold dear, close to our hearts, and perhaps they are our best friends that help us through whatever is happening be it good or not so good. Sometimes they are so close to us that they become a part of who we are. Sometimes they have names and sometimes they do not. This does not mean we have split personalities, no, no, this is not what is intended here. They are just that part of us that is on the inside and not on the outside, but that gives us the feeling of being brave if we are not, bold if we are not, joyful if we are not, happy if we are not.

Whatever we are not, they become that part. It is a good thing. It is also part of the protection we provide ourselves for whatever the reasons which are usually unbeknownst to us at the time.

Mary e.Stewart

I have watched throughout the years, children and their unseen, silent friends if you will and what happens for them. I have watched grandchildren go through the same thing. I do believe that children see things that adults do not see as they are so pure and innocent without any of the barriers that society puts in our way. Some of their wisdoms come from beyond what their young years of experience could possibly give them. It does make one sit back and take a deeper look at human beings as a whole, if only we would take the time to explore.

Mary e. Stewart

There are many parts or sides to most people, we are not just a single composition. We are a blank canvas if you will waiting to be painted or a tapestry waiting to be woven with all of the colors of the rainbow.

Many years ago, I was teasing my husband unmercifully and he asked me "Who is it that makes you do this?" I looked him straight away in the eyes without hesitation and said "Margaret, it is Margaret who does these things, because, well, Mary never would". He looked at me with much disbelief and started laughing because it was true.

Margaret has allowed me the spontaneity of the moment, bringing that part to the surface without hesitation and without fear of reprisal. Since then, I have been known to be called either Mary Margaret or just Margaret. She is the fun part of me, the mischievous part of me, and the joyful part of me. She is the funny one with a great sense of humor who laughs at her own jokes when no one else does. She is the one who likes the crowds and is not afraid to be on stage at any time. She is an important part of me. **She brings the balance.**

Mary e.Stewart

Please do not misunderstand me, Mary has quite the sense of humor and sees the light side of most things. She is organized in her mind and understands more than most without much ado. She is the one who sees what is really happening with people even when they do not. She is the one who will be there when no one else would and will help you through almost anything if she is capable. She also knows her limits and can be very serious when needed. She will not interfere when she knows it is not in the best interest of whomever.

She trusts, especially in herself and what she knows beyond the superficial. She as well as Margaret is very spiritual and believes with her whole being in God and his teachings, but she is not a "sell it by zealot", and leaves each to their own beliefs. **As it should be.**

Yet, somewhere along the way in the last few years, Margaret has gone missing, and Mary is looking for her. She is not frantic yet because she knows that one can miss the clues and understandings when this happens. She is looking. Yes, she is definitely searching and feels the emptiness of having Margaret missing.

Mary e.Stewart

So how do we find Margaret? Where is she and why has she gone missing.
Are there any clues?

I guess we have to take a long look at what has happened in the last ever
many years in Mary's life and sort out the information. A mystery for
sure, or is it. Perhaps it is just life and the difficult things that take place,
placing no blame on one thing or any one person. Hopefully we take
responsibility of our lives, yet sometimes circumstances play such a
huge role, outcomes are taken out of our hands and we lose sight of our
emotional well beings for a while.

It is easy to buy into what society has taught us and put our own unique
belief system to the side....for a while. When we do find our balance is off,
our feet are not touching the ground so we become ungrounded, it can be
dizzying and the result is ....**Margaret goes missing.**

Mary e.Stewart

So what are the clues, what is the information and are we willing to take a good look into what is happening for us now and events that have led us here. Margaret is missing and there really is no choice except to find her, and because she is missing a large part of Mary is missing.

The dictionary defines clue as "something that leads out of a perplexity. A fact or object that helps to solve a problem or mystery". So we dig a little deeper and find out what happened to make Margaret go missing.

Perhaps we do not need to know everything and just knowing she is missing and the willingness to take a good look is a great beginning.

Mary e.Stewart

We all have issues with jobs, family or friends, life, at one time or another and if taken one by one and breaking it down perhaps it would become a little easier to decipher the chain of events.

There are many milestones in our lives and they are defined in different ways, we are born, we turn 5 and then we turn 10. Turning 13 is impacting on all of us because suddenly we are teens or tweens and are we ready for it?

Probably not, but what can you do except be 13. Just get through it, your body changing, your emotions changing, growing taller and being gangly or not growing at all and staying the same that year. It can be like having a bad hair day every day with no end in sight. Turning 16 is another milestone and the Margaret of our lives begins a journey to the surface in a larger way. She becomes more visible.

Mary e. Stewart

You turn 18, a huge milestone, and no longer just a high school student, you are about to embark into the adult world, like it or not. Quickly thrown into that world complete with all of the joys and consequences of running your own life. Perhaps college is here now and you are studying for a career you have always wanted or your parents wanted for you, then graduation is here and you discover jobs are not so easy to find.

Your parents warned you to not take only general courses, but to specialize so you could be more than just well rounded. You were trying to follow the "not so good advice of the college councilors" and not specializing in the beginning. Somehow you knew in today's world it would be best to be specialized in something. Whose advice did you follow?

Yet when Margaret was there, life's traumas were not quite so dramatic, even with no job; and somehow Margaret and all that she represented cut through the drama and you came out okay landing on your feet.

Mary e.Stewart

Perhaps the next step is you get married, begin a family and step into a whole new world. Another chapter. You gather your family up and bring them into a supportive world of love and hope as you know it. Learning about the ups and downs of becoming a mother or a father. You are supportive and respectful of one another and dream of always being together, always.

Yet life does not always give us what we dream of, in the way we dream, and it takes a lot of understanding of each other to walk through any diversity that may come along. Sometimes it works and sometimes it does not. When it does work, it can be a wonderful thing and yet when it does not there can be a lot of heartache working its way through and seeps into one's being.

Again, Margaret is there to help guide and weave the way through the tough times, if only we will let her, she has so much to offer.

Mary e. Stewart

No one has ever said it would be easy, it is the human experience of everyday living and learning along the way. We learn why communication is so important and having that communication in a good way with the ones you love, people you are around and anyone you come into contact with, is imperative.

When the communication becomes hazy or misunderstood, and you believe you are not listened to or heard, plus if you are not listening and hearing, then things happen that we do not want to happen. We begin to listen less to Margaret and more to the chaos that seems to be surrounding us as we fall into the trap that society presents and we fail to sort it all out in a good way. Perhaps emotions are high and the sense of reason has also fallen to the wayside. Margaret is now missing. **We are not paying attention**.

Mary e.Stewart

So what are the clues, what will lead you out of this perplexity.......what is the answer or the beginning of a solution in finding Margaret?

Thinking back and taking a deeper look I see several issues that come to the forefront. Communication of wants and needs is one. The question becomes, are we allowed to feed and nourish our own wants and needs? Are we allowed to say what we want and need out loud? Will we be heard if we express our needs or will we just blow in the wind like the tall grass in the meadows during a storm?

Mary e.Stewart

Sometimes expressing wants and needs can be misconstrued as being selfish. Selfish means, according to the dictionary, that "one is too concerned with one's own welfare or interests and having little or no concern for others. Being self-centered." It is a word to be used carefully. Expressing your needs and wants in a good way is a form of loving yourself, it is not a selfish thing. It is the opposite and has a beautiful effect on all you come in contact with.

When you communicate what your wants and needs are to those around you and do it in a good way, letting others know what is important to you, it can be a freeing and beautiful thing. Especially if you are heard and you are given the respect of having been listened to, with no interruptions or judgments. Yet when you feel you are not being heard and listened to with good intent, (remember it does not matter what the other person was thinking or intending), **your perception** is that you were not being listened to, not heard. It hurts, causes grief and is difficult to sort out with clarity and can bring resentment.

Mary e. Stewart

Yet when Margaret is there, she helps with understanding and with all of the gifts she possesses, joy, love, understanding, clarity, and peacefulness, she walks you through the issues. It happens in a split second, a thought or knowing that it is not you. It does not matter what others think or what their judgments may be just do not hold onto their judgments and let them change part of who you are. I am not saying to lie down and be walked on or just accept the other person's viewpoint. I am saying you have validity in what you are sharing. What you have shared is very important and it takes courage to do this. However the other person receives or handles what you have shared is their path, and frankly has nothing to do with you. It is all of their own "stuff". This is one of those times when we need Margaret the most, and now she seems to be missing and we are stuck.

So, where is Margaret and how do we find her? How do we handle these situations and not go into chaos bumping against the walls because either someone will talk over us, or not take into consideration what we have said. Whatever is happening does not seem to fit into their understanding and my guess is they probably think they are not being listened to as well. Seems to me it could be a "catch 22".

Mary e. Stewart

Mary Stewart

Finding Margaret is all important because when she is around, everything seems to go right, things fit into place. Not only for fun, but for everyday living because she sees the goodness, the humor, the seriousness, attitude, the self-worth, the loving of self and others. She only sees the positive and does not see the negative. She oversees the competence we feel, how we handle business and how we attain business. **She is the balance** and because of her, situations seem lighter unless we cannot find her.

Dig deeper. Let go of what others think; accept who you are; realize that you are okay and above all, love yourself. **All Priceless.**

Mary e.Stewart

So here it is. In personal relationships, and in the whole scheme of things, it does not really matter if people cannot see your humor, or if they do not accept who you are and always have been. It does not matter if they approve or disapprove of how you handle things because it is not their way. It does not matter if they fail to say nice things such as "you look really great today, or I appreciate you, or saying I love you in a heartfelt way. It surely would be wonderful if the loving and caring things were said, but you and Margaret know who you are and can see beyond the unsaid. You have the knowingness to look beyond and understand and appreciate who others are. When one has understanding it is really difficult to be mad for long and it is all because you understand what is happening. Just a warm thank you can mean everything, and also mean the same to someone else when you say it from the heart.

Mary e.Stewart

When we are feeling or seeing the disappointment that others may have in us, it would be valuable to understand that it is not us that has disappointed but perhaps it is the expectations of others that are unattainable. You know instinctively if they have a right to be disappointed because you did not do what you said or promised you would do. If something is your fault, then it is your fault and you can do something to change that.

People who really love and care for you do not stop loving or caring or give up on you because you did not live up to what they had hoped. You should not continually beat yourself up for having done things you wish you had not done, or continually walk on the proverbial eggshells. **It is not healthy**.

People who really love and care for you do not hold the past hostage for what they may think you have done wrong. They do not relive and live in the past. One cannot move forward and live in the today while living in the past. **It is impossible**.

Mary e. Stewart

Hopefully they work their own way through their experience and learn forgiveness and trust, that is part of learning what love is. We experience this all the time, all of us do and sometimes it is just our own perception that someone is disappointed, but this is where Margaret comes in again. She helps us go through these situations and come out whole on the other end. She helps us sort through. **She is the understanding and the balance.**

How do we find Margaret, the same question? The answers might come by taking a look at self, changing attitude, meditating, praying, asking for forgiveness and giving forgiveness. Asking for help from whatever source we need. Finding quiet time, which for me happens to be painting. Looking for the joy of everyday life and the beauty of nature.

Acceptance and rejection to anger, trying to find a solution and a different path to understanding. No feeling sorry for self, no reason to be there and becoming a victim. Exercise, walking, being in nature, not buying into someone else's anger, pain, negativity, hopelessness, absence of joy, or victimization and letting it become our own.

These things are easy for us to do but not when Margaret is around, she knows how to navigate the way through this maze.

Mary e.Stewart

Mary Stewart ©

When taking the time to look into what we are feeling we begin to open a door that we had perhaps closed unknowingly. A door that leads to the world of understanding, mostly of self, the joy and peace that follows. A world where once again we love ourselves and do not beat ourselves up for any reason, where we are not afraid of the unknown but welcome it in to explore and investigate. My experience has been that I know in my heart and whole being that I am one with God. He is always with me and the purpose of my journey on this earth is to be one with Him and live my life in the best way I know how. I understand and know that part of my journey is being there for others without expectations and without having to voice what I have done in the world. That is not important. **He knows**.

Mary e. Stewart

So where is Margaret?   As my oldest daughter Brenda, at the young and wise age of 20, said to me many years ago, "Mom you have been searching so long and hard trying to find yourself and what you did not realize is that you were here all along." Enough to make any mom cry, I think she knows Margaret.

I do believe after this soul searching adventure that Margaret never really disappeared or went missing. She has been standing back giving me the opportunity to grow once more and become more of who I am, a constant never ending adventure that is still ongoing.

 I am grateful for my adventure and I am hopeful if you have a Margaret that has gone missing you will soon have your own soul searching adventure and bring her home.

Mary e.Stewart

So Margaret welcome home,

You were not missing, only standing back in the wings of the stage our lives are played out on. Only for a short time were you missing in the drama I call my life.

Welcome Home and on to the next adventure.

Remember your life is an occasion....rise to it,

Find your Margaret if it seems as though

She has gone missing,

Perhaps she has really been there all along.

Mary e. Stewart

Mary Stewart